EVERYONE TOOTS

Everyone Toots

JOE Rhatigan • Illustrated by Alejandro O'Kif

Teacher toots during playtime,
when she thinks no one is near.

But it makes quite a sound
that all the students hear.

As the band plays their instruments, the crowd hears a weird trombone. There are no horns! It's the drummer tooting near a microphone.

Grandpa toots near Grandma,
who doesn't hear the racket.

But then she covers up her nose
with her pretty purple jacket.

A hippo and an elephant
make bubbles in the lake.
If you're standing close enough,
it makes your body shake.

A unicorn toot smells like candy
and freshly fallen snow.
Instead of stinky clouds and fumes,
it makes a sparkly rainbow.

The King and Queen of Tootland
can toot loudly without fear.
All the court must pretend
they never even hear.

The batter swings and misses,
and then lets out a sound.
You can smell the gas he made
on the pitcher's mound.

The ballerina jumps and twirls
and lets a toot go free.
She looks around the stage and says,
"Hey, that wasn't me!"

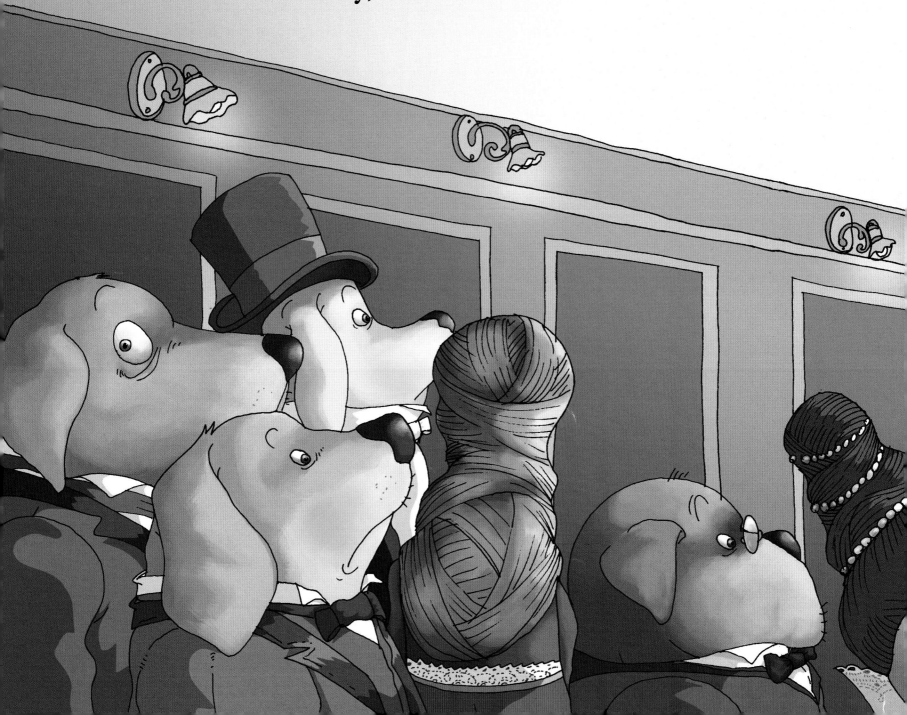

A handsome prince once tried to give
Sleeping Beauty a kiss.
A rumbling roar from Beauty's rear
made the poor prince miss.

The astronaut tried not to,
but then she had to toot.
The gas had nowhere else to go
and filled her whole spacesuit.

don't worry about a toot or two
—because it happens to everyone!

The End

Brimming with creative inspiration, how-to projects, and useful information to enrich your everyday life, Quarto Knows is a favorite destination for those pursuing their interests and passions. Visit our site and dig deeper with our books into your area of interest: Quarto Creates, Quarto Cooks, Quarto Homes, Quarto Lives, Quarto Drives, Quarto Explores, Quarto Gifts, or Quarto Kids.

© 2017 Quarto Publishing Group USA Inc.

First Published in 2017 by MoonDance Press, an imprint of The Quarto Group.
6 Orchard Road, Suite 100, Lake Forest, CA 92630, USA.
T (949) 380-7510 **F** (949) 380-7575 **www.QuartoKnows.com**

MoonDance Press titles are also available at discount for retail, wholesale, promotional, and bulk purchase. For details, contact the Special Sales Manager by email at specialsales@quarto.com or by mail at The Quarto Group, Attn: Special Sales Manager, 401 Second Avenue North, Suite 310, Minneapolis, MN 55401 USA.

ISBN: 978-1-63322-224-3

Illustrations by Alejandro O'Kif
Cover design and layout by Melissa Gerber

Printed in China
10 9 8 7 6 5 4 3 2 1